CHAMELEONS

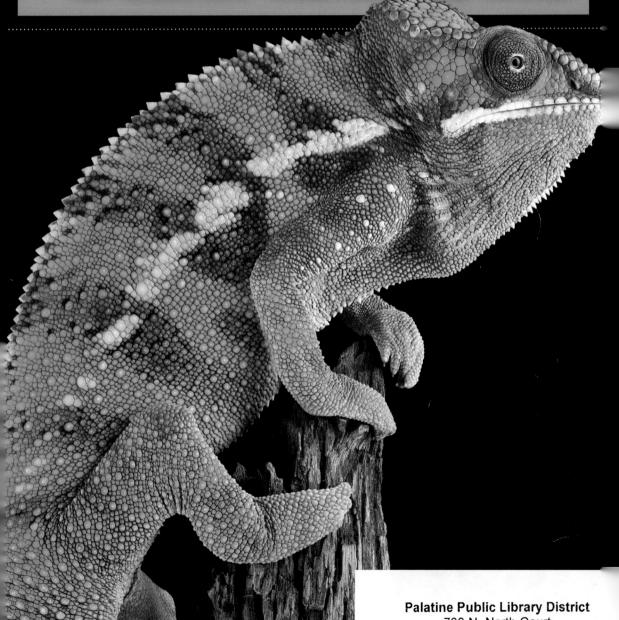

BY PETER MURRA

The Child's World®

Published by The Child's World®
1980 Lookout Drive • Mankato, MN 56003-1705
800-599-READ • www.childsworld.com

ACKNOWLEDGMENTS
The Child's World®: Mary Berendes, Publishing Director
Olivia Gregory: Editing
Pamela J. Mitsakos: Photo Research

PHOTO CREDITS
© bluedogroom/Shutterstock.com: 17; CathyKeifer/iStock.com: cover, 1,
13; davemhuntphotography/Shutterstock.com: 7; EmmyD/Shutterstock.
com: 1; fivespots/Shutterstock.com: 15; Larusov/Dreamstime.com: 20;
Marek Velechovsky/Shutterstock.com: 5; PhotoDisc: 23, 24; Ryan M.
Bolton/Shutterstock.com: 9; skydie/Shutterstock.com: 10

ISBN 9781631437038
LCCN 2014945315

Printed in the United States of America
Mankato, MN
November, 2014
PA02242

ABOUT THE AUTHOR

Peter Murray has written more than 80 children's books on science, nature, history, and other topics. He also writes novels for adults and teens under the name Pete Hautman. An animal lover, Pete lives in Golden Valley, Minnesota, in a house with one woman, two poodles, several dozen spiders, thousands of microscopic dust mites, and an occasional mouse.

TABLE OF CONTENTS

On the cover: Panther chameleons like this one live on the island of Madagascar.

MEET THE CHAMELEON!

Unlike our eyes (which move together), a chameleon's eyes move separately. This means they can see in two different directions at the same time.

Chameleons have been around for about 60 million years.

Somewhere in Africa, a creature sits on a tree branch, waiting and watching. Its long toes grip the branch, and its tail is coiled like a spring. Its pebbly skin is mottled green and brown. Its body is flat, like a leaf. The only things moving are its cone-shaped eyes.

The creature takes a very slow step forward. It looks as if it is moving in slow motion! It slowly turns its head and opens its mouth. *ZOT!* The creature's tongue shoots out and hits an insect, bringing it back to the creature's mouth. What is this strange animal? It's a chameleon!

Veiled chameleons like this one live in the mountain areas of Yemen, the United Arab Emirates, and Saudi Arabia.

COLOR CHANGERS

People used to think that chameleons change color to blend in with their surroundings. We know now that this is not true. Instead, they change color in response to temperature or mood.

It takes about 20 seconds for a chameleon to change colors.

Chameleons belong to a group of **reptiles** called **lizards**. Lizards are related to the dinosaurs that one ruled Earth. Like all reptiles, lizards have **scales** instead of feathers or hair. They are also **cold blooded**—their body temperature rises and falls with the temperature of the air around them. When a chameleon is too cold, it moves even more slowly than usual. It crawls sluggishly into sunlight to warm itself. When it gets too hot, the chameleon heads for cool shadows.

When a chameleon's body temperature changes, a strange thing happens—its skin changes color, too! Most chameleons are brown or green—but not always! In hot weather, some chameleons turn black and gray. When the temperature cools, their normal color returns. A chameleon's color also changes when it is angry, afraid, or excited. The chameleon might get darker, or red and yellow spots might appear.

Panther chameleons like this one can grow to be 20 inches (51 cm) long.

WARM-AREA ANIMALS

Half of the world's chameleons live on the island of Madagascar.

Chameleons can sleep upside down.

Madagascar's *Brookesia micra* chameleon is the world's smallest chameleon species.

The *Malagasy giant chameleon*, also from Madagascar, is the world's largest chameleon species.

Chameleons live in Africa, India, parts of southern Europe, on the island of Madagascar, and along the Mediterranean coast. They live in warm areas where the sun can heat their bodies.

There are over 160 **species** of chameleons. Some have horns and look like miniature dinosaurs. Some have spines on their backs or under their chins. Others have crests on the tops of their heads. The smallest chameleon is less than an inch (2.5 cm) long. Most chameleons are five or six inches long, but some grow to be much larger. The biggest chameleon can grow to be over two feet long!

Brown leaf chameleons got their name because they look like a dead brown leaf. These tiny chameleons live in Madagascar and only grow to be about 3 inches (8 cm) long.

LIFE IN THE TREES

Chameleons spend most of their lives in trees. Their feet are made for climbing and are not much good for walking on the ground. Each foot looks like the jaws of a pair of pliers, with three toes on one side and two on the other. Chameleons use their feet to grasp small branches. They can also use them like hands to pull bad-tasting insects out of their mouths.

A chameleon's tail is also designed for life in the trees. Other lizards can move their tails back and forth or up and down, but only a chameleon can coil its tail around a branch and hang from it! Chameleons use their tails for climbing, balancing, or just hanging around.

Because they move so slowly, chameleons are always in danger of being eaten by larger animals. To survive, they rely on their **camouflage**—but camouflage does not always work. A chameleon confronted by a bird, large lizard, or a snake will change color and **inflate** its lungs to make itself look bigger. The horns and spines on some chameleons make them look larger and fiercer than they really are. Sometimes this discourages **predators**—but not often enough!

Each toe on a chameleon has a claw to help grip surfaces when climbing.

Snakes and birds are the most common chameleon predators.

Chameleons are **diurnal**, which means they are active during the daytime and sleep at night.

You can see this veiled chameleon's feet and tail as it walks on a branch.

EATING EVERYTHING

Some larger chameleon species will eat smaller reptiles.

A chameleon can shoot its tongue at almost 13 miles (21 km) per hour.

Chameleons have excellent eyesight. They can see small insects up to 33 feet (10 m) away.

A chameleon's tongue expands at the end, turning it into a kind of "suction cup" to catch food.

Chameleons eat almost anything, from insects, spiders, and worms to snails, berries, and fruit.

The chameleon is a sluggish animal, but it has a very fast, very long tongue. Some chameleons have tongues that are longer than their bodies! When its tongue is not in use, the chameleon keeps it bunched up inside its mouth. But when it spies an insect, the chameleon opens its mouth and flexes its powerful tongue muscles. The tongue shoots out so fast you can hardly see it! The end of the tongue, which is coated with **mucus**, sticks to the insect. In a flash, the insect is yanked back into the chameleon's mouth. Crunch! To the chameleon, an insect is better than pepperoni pizza!

This young veiled chameleon has just caught a fly with its tongue.

FIGHTING

Male chameleons often have more horns, bumps, and spikes than females. This helps when they fight other males.

Some chameleons can make a hissing or squeaking sound—but at a level human ears can't hear.

Chameleons prefer to live alone. During mating season, however, chameleons seek the company of other chameleons—except males, that is. Male chameleons often have wild fights over females.

When two male chameleons meet, a fight will often start. They hiss at each other and puff up their bodies. They try to knock each other out of the way. When one male decides he has had enough, his skin turns dark, and he runs away. The winner then approaches the female. He can tell by the female's color if she is ready to mate.

This male Werner's chameleon is trying to frighten away the photographer. He has puffed himself up and opened his mouth. Werner's chameleons live in Tanzania.

LAYING EGGS

Some chameleon species can lay up to 100 eggs at one time.

While most chameleons lay eggs, a few species give birth to live babies.

After the chameleons mate, eggs inside the female's body begin to grow. When she is ready to lay her eggs, the female chameleon travels down the trunk of her tree. Chameleons do not like to leave their trees, but most species must lay their eggs underground.

The female chameleon digs a hole and lays a **clutch** of about 20 tiny eggs. She then covers them with dirt and climbs back into her tree. From then on the baby chameleons are on their own.

This newly hatched panther chameleon is crawling on the unhatched egg of its brother or sister.

CHAMELEON BABIES

Baby chameleons develop slowly inside their leathery eggshells. For some species, it can take almost a year for the eggs to hatch! Once a baby is fully developed, it cuts through its shell with a special **egg tooth**, then digs its way to the surface.

Chameleons start looking for small insects almost as soon as they hatch. No one is there to feed them, so they must learn to catch their own dinner! Life is dangerous for these tiny lizards, and many of them are eaten by birds and other animals before they reach full size.

Depending on the species, it can take between 4 and 12 months for a baby chameleon to hatch.

Like other lizards, baby chameleons **shed** their skin as they grow. The older, smaller skin dries up and falls off, revealing a newer, larger skin underneath.

This baby Cape dwarf chameleon is on its own. Cape dwarf chameleons live in South Africa, near Cape Town.

STAYING WILD

Pet chameleons can live up to 10 years. Wild chameleons live about 5 years.

Because of their strange appearance and their ability to change color, chameleons are often sold as pets. In Africa and Madagascar, chameleons are captured and shipped to other countries. But chameleons are difficult to keep in captivity, and few pet chameleons survive.

If too many chameleons are taken from the wild, and if we do not take care of the places in which they live, some species might disappear forever. Chameleons are happiest when they are left in the wild, where they can explore their tree branches, eat insects, and, when they are in the mood, change the color of their skin.

This big panther chameleon has changed to a bright color to warn the photographer to stay away.

GLOSSARY

camouflage (KAM-oo-flazh) Camouflage is special coloring or markings that helps an animal blend in with its surroundings. Chameleons have camouflage.

clutch (KLUTCH) A clutch is a group of eggs produced by an animal at the same time.

cold blooded (KOLD BLUD-ed) Cold-blooded animals are those that need outside heat to warm their bodies. Chameleons are cold blooded.

diurnal (dy-UR-null) An animal that is diurnal is active mostly during the day and rests at night. Chameleons are diurnal.

egg tooth (EGG TOOTH) An egg tooth is a hard bump that baby birds and reptiles grow on their beaks or noses to help them break out of their eggs. Baby chameleons have an egg tooth.

inflate (in-FLAYT) To inflate something is to puff it up by filling it with air. Chameleons inflate their lungs to make themselves look bigger.

lizards (LIZ-urdz) A lizard is a reptile that has a long body, legs, and a long, pointed tail. Chameleons are lizards.

mucus (MYOO-kuss) Mucus is a wet slime produced by some animals' bodies.

predators (PRED-uh-turz) Predators are animals that hunt and kill other animals for food.

reptiles (REP-tylz) Reptiles are animals that have backbones, lungs, and tough skin covered with scales, and that need outside heat to warm their bodies. Chameleons are reptiles.

scales (SKAYLZ) Scales are small, hard plates that cover some animals' skins. Chameleons have scales.

shed (SHED) When an animal sheds, it loses its old skin. Baby chameleons shed their skin as they grow.

species (SPEE-sheez) An animal species is a group of animals that share the same features and have babies only with animals in the same group. There are over 160 species of chameleons.

TO FIND OUT MORE

Read It!

Berne, Emma Carlson. *Chameleons: Masters of Disguise!* New York: PowerKids Press, 2014.

Gish, Melissa. *Chameleons.* Mankato, MN: Creative Education, 2013.

Lockwood, Sophie. *Chameleons.* Mankato, MN: The Child's World, 2006.

Schmidt, W., K. Tamm, and E. Wallikewitz. *Chameleons.* Philadelphia, PA: Chelsea House Publishers, 1999.

On the Web

Visit our home page for lots of links about chameleons:
www.childsworld.com/links

Note to Parents, Teachers, and Librarians: We routinely check our Web links to make sure they're safe, active sites—so encourage your readers to check them out!

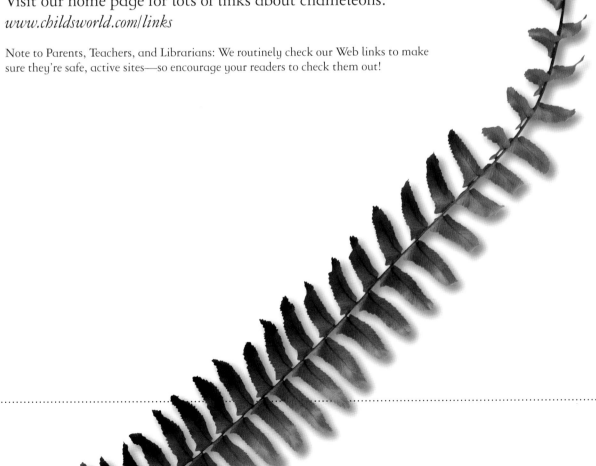

INDEX